# Muslim Poems
# for
# Children

Mymona Hendricks

The Islamic Foundation

© The Islamic Foundation 1991/1412 H. Reprinted 1996/1417 H. and 2004

ISBN 0 86037 218 9

# MUSLIM CHILDREN'S LIBRARY

General Editors:
**M. Manazir Ahsan** and **Anwar Cara**

# MUSLIM POEMS FOR CHILDREN

Author: **Mymona Hendricks**

Cover design and illustrations: **Anwar Cara**

*Published by*
The Islamic Foundation,
Markfield Dawah Centre,
Ratby Lane, Markfield,
Leicester LE67 9RN,
United Kingdom.

Quran House
P.O. Box 30611,
Nairobi, Kenya.

P.M.B. 3193
Kano, Nigeria.

British Library Cataloguing in Publication Data

Hendricks, Mymona
    Muslim poems for children. – (Muslim children's library)
    I. Title II. Series
    811.54
    ISBN 0 86037 218 9

Printed by Ashford Colour Press Ltd, Gosport, Hants.

# MUSLIM CHILDREN'S LIBRARY

## An Introduction

Here is a new series of books, but with a difference, for children of all ages. Published by the Islamic Foundation, the Muslim Children's Library has been produced to provide young people with something they cannot perhaps find anywhere else.

Most of today's children's books aim only to entertain and inform or to teach some necessary skills, but not to develop the inner and moral resources. Entertainment and skills by themselves impart nothing of value to life unless a child is also helped to discover deeper meaning in himself and the world around him. Yet there is no place in them for God, Who alone gives meaning to life and the universe, nor for the divine guidance brought by His prophets, following which can alone ensure an integrated development of the total personality.

Such books, in fact, rob young people of access to true knowledge. They give them no unchanging standards of right and wrong, nor any incentives to live by what is right and refrain from what is wrong. The result is that all too often the young enter adult life in a state of social alienation and bewilderment, unable to cope with the seemingly unlimited choices of the world around them. The situation is especially devastating for the Muslim child as he may grow up cut off from his culture and values.

The Muslim Children's Library aspires to remedy this deficiency by showing children the deeper meaning of life and the world around them; by pointing them along paths leading to an integrated development of all aspects of their personality; by helping to give them the capacity to cope with the complexities of their world, both personal and social; by opening vistas into a world extending far beyond this life; and, to a Muslim child especially, by providing a fresh and strong faith, a dynamic commitment, an indelible sense of identity, a throbbing yearning and an urge to struggle, all rooted in Islam. The books aim to help a child anchor his development on the rock of divine guidance, and to understand himself and relate to himself and others in just and meaningful ways. They relate directly to his soul and intellect, to his emotions and imagination, to his motives and desires, to his anxieties and hopes - indeed, to every aspect of his fragile, but potentially rich personality. At the same time it is recognized that for a book to hold a child's attention, he must enjoy reading it; it should therefore arouse his curiosity and entertain him as well. The style, the language, the illustrations and the production of the books are all geared to this goal. They provide moral education, but not through sermons or ethical abstractions.

Although these books are based entirely on Islamic teachings and the vast Muslim heritage, they should be of equal interest and value to all children, whatever their country or creed; for Islam is a universal religion, the natural path.

Adults, too, may find much of use in them. In particular, Muslim parents and teachers will find that they provide what they have for so long been so badly needing. The books will include texts on the Qur'an, the *Sunnah* and other basic sources and teachings of Islam, as well as history, stories and anecdotes for supplementary reading. The books are presented with full colour illustrations keeping in view the limitations set by Islam. Along the lines of our *Muslim Nursery Rhymes* the present book, a collection of poems, aims at inculcating in Muslim children the message and teaching of Islam.

We invite parents and teachers to use these books in homes and classrooms, at breakfast tables and bedsides and encourage children to derive maximum benefit from them. At the same time their greatly valued observations and suggestions are highly welcome.

To the young reader we say: You hold in your hands books which may be entirely different from those you have been reading till now, but we sincerely hope you will enjoy them; try, through these books, to understand yourself, your life, your experiences and the universe around you. They will open before your eyes new paths and models in life that you will be curious to explore and find exciting and rewarding to follow. May God be with you forever.

We are grateful to everyone who has helped us in the preparation of this book, particularly Dr. A.R. Kidwai, Br. Sarwar Rija and Br. Faiyazuddin Ahmad, who read the poems with great interest and offered valuable suggestions. We also thank the author for ungrudgingly accepting our suggestions and changing the manuscript more than once.

May Allah bless with His mercy and acceptance our humble contribution to the urgent and gigantic task of producing books for a new generation of children, a task which we have undertaken in all humility and hope.

**M. Manazir Ahsan**
**Director General**

4

# Contents

# Who am I?

I have much reason to rejoice,
And praise Allah in a grateful voice,
Because I'm happy and content,
With all the favours Allah sent.

He created me so perfectly,
And did it all so lovingly,
While showing me the way to go,
No wonder that I love Him so.

Therefore to Him I bow and pray,
And try to obey Him every day,
While believing in His Prophets too,
Who came to show us what to do.

In Allah's Books I do believe,
And in the Guidance I receive,
And I believe in His Angels too,
Who have special things to do.

One more thing I'd like to say,
There'll be another life one day,
And this I do believe my friend,
That death is not the final end.

So I am a  Muslim, as you can see,
A special person, you must agree,
That's who I am and I'm so proud,
I feel like saying it loud and loud.

# Shahadah

Declare the Oneness of Allah,
*La ilaha illal Lah,*
Allah is one and can't be three,
The truth is simple as can be.

He's the source of everything,
And doesn't need a single thing,
He wasn't born and will not die,
And that is surely not a lie.

*Muhammad-ur-Rasulullah,*
The final Prophet of Allah,
Peace and blessings on him too,
Who came to show us what to do.

Allah chose him for mankind,
No one greater will we find,
And his *Sunnah* is our guide,
By his ways we should abide.

Those who believe in Allah now,
Must accept this simple vow,
*La ilaha illal Lah,*
*Muhammad-ur-Rasulullah,*

This *Shahadah* is a sacred creed,
Live by it and you'll succeed,
And be a witness to the truth,
Though you be a child or youth.

There is no god but Allah

Muhammad is the Messenger of Allah

# Servants of Allah

In toil and struggle we were created,
Made from clay for a term appointed,
Servants of Allah we then became,
Both men and women just the same.

To us was given a special Trust,
Submission to Him became a must,
Shunning the bad while doing good,
Pleasing Allah as Muslims should.

Our every action should portray,
The *Din* of Islam that is our way,
To Allah's Will we all must bow,
Because we are His servants now.

Those most pious are the best,
Believers who just never rest,
They sacrifice and they endure,
For Allah's pleasure to ensure.

We'll make mistakes as we go along,
By sometimes doing things that are wrong,
But Allah forgives if we repent,
When our regret is truly meant.

So Allah chose us all you see,
And that includes both you and me,
So let us prove what we are worth,
We are His servants on this earth.

# The Holy Qur'an

The Qur'an is a Mercy and a Light,
Guiding mankind to what is right,
And also a Blessing and a Sign,
With teachings that are so Divine,
While it leads us to salvation,
And warns us against temptation.

This Revelation for all time,
Which no doubt is so sublime,
Is for people of every race,
Sent to us by Allah's Grace,
Explaining what we ought to do,
While it is a Healing too.

It tells of Allah's Attributes,
While idol-worship it refutes,
With warnings of a terrible day,
For those of us who go astray,
And calls us to repent you know,
While showing us the way to go.

And the meaning and the Message,
As we read through every passage,
Can touch our very heart and soul,
Leading us towards our goal,

And inner happiness we will find,
When reading with an open mind.

The Qur'an is alive and so are we,
So turn to it and you will see,
That it's unique in every way,
Despite what some of the people say,
For the Qur'an is our guiding light,
We must study it with all our might.

# Your Qur'an

How this big earth came to be,
And everything that we see,
Even things in outer space,
Came about by Allah's Grace....
Read it up in your Qur'an,
It will strengthen your *Iman*.

How people lived so long ago,
Lessons that we have to know,
And who does Allah love the best,
And why He puts us all to test....
Read it up in your Qur'an,
It will strengthen your *Iman*.

How He makes the raindrops fall,
And what about the trees so tall,
And the different plants that grow,
And reasons for the wind to blow....
Read it up in your Qur'an,
It will strengthen your *Iman*.

And what about the oceans wide,
And the animals that we ride,
Not to mention mountains high,
And magnificence of the sky....

Read it up in your Qur'an,
It will strengthen your *Iman*.

To find out what we mustn't do,
Things that are bad for me and you,
Also about the things that are right,
And how we all can gain insight....
Read it up in your Qur'an,
It will strengthen your *Iman*.

And the nature and the glory,
Unfolds like a beautiful story,
Of the Almighty as He talks to you,
Conveying a Message pure and true....
Read it up in your Qur'an,
It will strengthen your *Iman*.

# The Prophet Muhammad
### (peace be upon him)

He was honest, truthful and very kind,
And the greatest teacher of mankind,
Who was exalted in his character too,
And never strayed from what is true,
Despite the obstacles that prevailed,
He struggled on and never failed.

And Muhammad is his blessed name,
Who called for *Tawhid* when he came,
And in the process suffered much,
But never lost his special touch,
Of being polite and kind and good,
And always called for brotherhood.

To everyone he brought much joy,
Though he was orphaned as a boy,
He always led a truthful life,
Despite the hardship and the strife,
For he was steadfast all the way,
Submitting to Allah every day.

He brought guidance so complete,
And taught us how to pray and eat,
While in the *Sunnah* you'll recall,
Are detailed teachings for us all,

And no more Prophets there will be,
For he's the final one, you see.

# The Five Pillars of Islam

Allah is One and like no one,
He has no partner, nor a son,
He is Kind and Just and Wise,
And has no form, shape or size.

His final Messenger to all of us,
Did so much without a fuss,
Muhammad is his blessed name,
As mercy to the worlds he came.

Five times a day we make *Salah,*
That's when we bow down to Allah,
We ask for guidance when we pray,
And this we do every single day.

We have to share with those in need,
And not give in to thoughts of greed,
*Zakah* then helps us in this way,
Lest we should err and go astray.

In the month of Ramadan we must fast,
From the first day to the last,
When food and drink we put aside,
By fasting rules we then abide.

And all those who can afford,
Seek the pleasure of their Lord,
They perform their *Hajj* you know,
When to Makkah the pilgrims go.

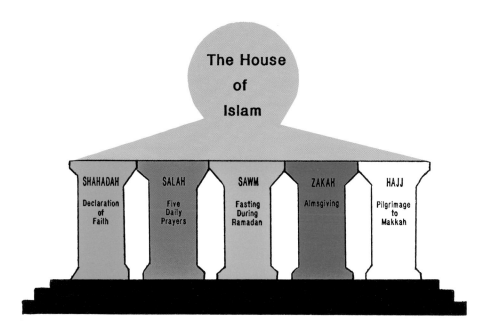

# ʿIbadah

As we live from day to day,
And try to strive in Allah's way,
It is known as *ʿIbadah* too,
It's what everyone must do.

What we think, talk and act,
Becomes *ʿIbadah* that's a fact,
If every effort that we make,
Is purely done for Allah's sake.

We might be tempted to disobey,
But we must make a choice today,
For life on earth is but a test,
And obeying Allah, is the best.

So therefore, it would be nice,
If Fasting, *Hajj* and Sacrifice,
And the performance of *Salah,*
Could bring us closer to Allah.

And sincere believers in *Tawhid,*
Are the ones who will succeed,
They know that Allah is so near,
He's the One that they fear.

So Muslims who are truly keen,
Follow the teachings of their *Din*,
While all the time remembering,
That *'Ibadah* touches everything.

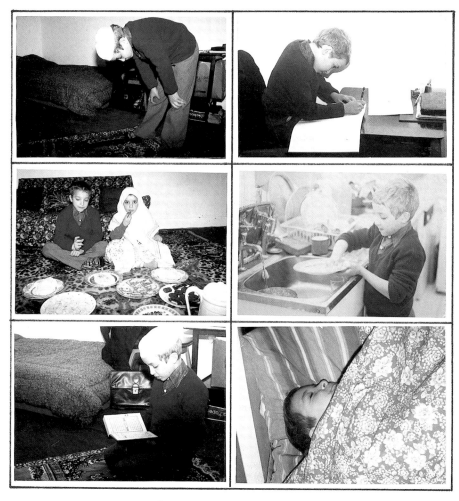

**Some acts of *'Ibadah***

# Wudu

The *Wudu* that all Muslims make,
Is an act of purity for Allah's sake,
To cleanse our body and our soul,
For to Allah is our final goal,
And therefore we must all be pure,
For He loves purity, that's for sure.

We also try to cleanse our hearts,
While washing certain body parts,
And this is how the pattern goes,
Hands and mouth and then the nose,
Then followed by the face you see,
It's as easy as can be.

Wash your arms to the elbow now,
I am sure, that you know how,
Wipe the head with a wet hand too,
Down to your neck, I'm telling you,
Then clean your ears and wash your feet,
This is how *Wudu* is complete.

But wash yourself in Allah's name,
And always you must do the same,
And don't forget the short *Du'a*,
For you must always praise Allah,

So any time you want to pray,
Just make *Wudu,* this easy way.

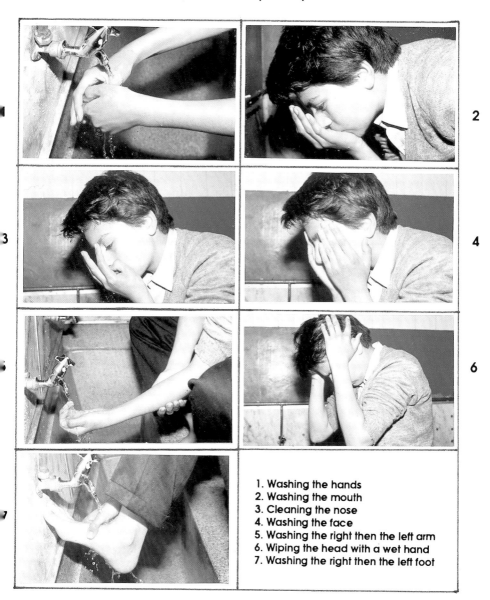

1. Washing the hands
2. Washing the mouth
3. Cleaning the nose
4. Washing the face
5. Washing the right then the left arm
6. Wiping the head with a wet hand
7. Washing the right then the left foot

23

# Salah

We worship Allah every day,
For He's the One we must obey,
So five times daily when we pray,
We ask Him to show us the Right Way.

We glorify and thank Allah,
Remembering Him in our *Salah,*
And while we do this we recall,
How Merciful He is to all.

Before the sun does rise each day,
It's *Fajr Salah* that we must pray,
And after mid-day we take a break,
To perform *Zuhr* for Allah's sake.

Late afternoon it's *'Asr* we pray,
A command by Allah we must obey,
We seek protection from His wrath,
And guidance to the Straight Path.

And after the sun has surely set,
There's *Maghrib* we must not forget,
And just before we go to bed,
There's *'Isha'* that must be read.

These acts of *'Ibadah* we uphold,
Have benefits that are manifold,
So let's submit and praise Allah,
For there's no Islam without *Salah*.

And *Salah* keeps us away from sin,
Increasing *Taqwa* and discipline,
Without it we'll be lost you see,
And true Muslims we would never be.

# The Rak'ah

Let me teach you something now,
Just in case you don't know how,
When you intend to make *Salah*,
And turn your face towards *Ka'bah*,
You must have your *Wudu* too,
It is the proper thing to do.

Lift your hands and say *Takbir*,
Just like this, my dear Munir,
Fold your hands while standing still,
Submit yourself to Allah's will,
Then you read the *Fatihah*,
Always thinking of Allah.

Then add a section from the Qur'an,
As praying builds up your *Iman*,
Now hands upon your knees you place,
While beseeching Allah's Grace,
That is when you make *Ruku'*,
Making you feel humble, too.

Then stand up in all humility,
And praise Allah with sincerity,
Then prostrate onto the floor,
Praising Allah more and more,

Sit again before *Sujud,*
Bow to Allah in gratitude.

You have made one *Rak'ah,*
A basic part of the *Salah,*
While obeying Allah's call,
A sacred duty on us all,
So you and I must always pray,
And bow to Allah every day.

# Fasting

We all must fast in Ramadan,
Which is one of the five *Arkan,*
It is a blessed month you know,
We fast for Allah, not for show.

It's designed to make us think,
As we refrain from food and drink,
We feel the hunger and the pain,
And much there is for us to gain.

From dawn till dusk we fast,
Hoping that our *Sawm* can last,
While we try to do much good,
Building *Taqwa* like we should.

Special prayers we say at night,
And turn to Allah in our plight,
To forgive and guide us as we try,
While ourselves we purify.

And remember it was in Ramadan,
When Allah revealed the Holy Qur'an,
And so began the Prophet's call,
A guide and mercy to us all.

And the night of *Qadr* is unique,
Its blessings all believers seek,
Then will follow the day of *'Id*,
A truly festive day indeed.

Fasting teaches discipline too,
And self-control for me and you,
As year by year we train to be,
Better Muslims, by Allah's decree.

**Believers! fasting is enjoined upon you, as it was enjoined upon those before you, that you become God-fearing.**
(Baqarah 2:183)

# Zakah

Everything that we have and own,
And all the favours we are shown,
Which we normally hold so dear,
Must be purified once a year.

For we are all just Trustees now,
Possessions are not ours somehow,
But Allah gave them for a while,
For all of us this is a trial.

So let us give the poor their due,
Which is a duty, that is true,
One of the Pillars or *Arkan,*
Which do support our *Iman.*

The traveller and the one in debt,
As well as destitutes can get,
The benefit of *Zakah* which leads,
To purity of wealth and deeds.

The receiver and the giver of aid,
All feel good when *Zakah* is paid,
And society as a whole will be,
Enriched by acts of charity.

So one thing we must understand,
It's always good to lend a hand,
For *Zakah* uplifts us all my friend,
And everyone benefits in the end.

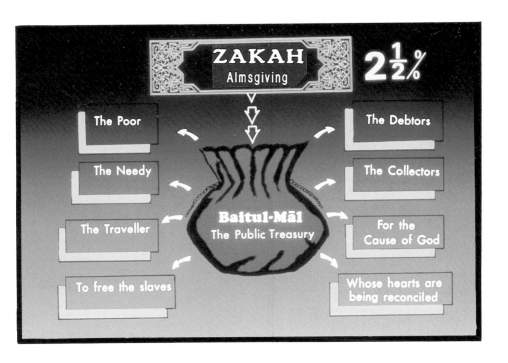

# Hajj

This sacred journey we undertake,
Is purely done for Allah's sake,
But when to Makkah Muslims go,
They must have the means you know,
And the *Hajj* will have more benefit,
For Pilgrims who are physically fit.

They'll see the *Ka'bah* or Baitullah,
Which is the *Qiblah* in our *Salah*,
They will wear *Ihram* you see,
Make *Tawaf* and perform *Sa'i*,
Which are rituals they must make,
While the *Hajj* they undertake.

And at Arafat they will meet,
Despite the blazing sun and heat,
And the *Hajj* will reach its peak,
While Allah's Mercy pilgrims seek,
No matter what their colour or race,
To seek His pleasure and His Grace.

So much there is to learn and see,
When Muslims display such unity,
They who come from near and far,
And it doesn't matter who they are,

As long as Allah is their goal,
And they purify their soul.

Remember too, right from the start,
Virtues of each *Rukn* form part,
Of the *Hajj* in all its essence,
Not to mention all the lessons,
And the blessings without measure,
That we get by the Almighty's pleasure.

# Akhirah

What I'm telling you now is true,
Sometimes I don't know what to do,
When everything I do goes wrong,
Though I know I must be strong,
But then again life is a test,
And we must always do our best.

For everything we do and say,
While we live from day to day,
Including all things good and bad,
Which make us happy or make us sad,
Will be accounted for some day,
When we'll meet on Judgement Day.

Though each of us must surely die,
And you all know the reason why,
The One Who created us before,
Will bring us back to life once more,
And we'll all return back to Allah,
For eternal life in the *Akhirah*.

Loyal servants of Allah will find,
Eternal happiness and peace of mind,
For in the Hereafter they will know,
The presence of Allah Whom they love so,

And *Jannah* will be their dwelling place,
Where they will live by Allah's Grace.

But those who follow the devil's way,
Each one of them has gone astray,
And *Jahannam*, is where they will be,
They'll have fear and won't be free,
And miserable will be their stay,
And for their deeds they'll have to pay.

All this must come to pass one day,
So come my friend, do let us pray,
'O Allah, help us to prepare well,
And please protect us all from Hell,
Make us grow up good and wise,
And grant us a place in Paradise.'

And for him who fears the standing before his Lord will be two
gardens. Then which of the favours of your Lord will you deny.
(Al-Rahman 55:46)

# My Parents

Of all the people that I know,
Respect and honour I must show,
To Mother and to Father too,
For the wonderful things they do.

My Mother works so hard for me,
She is as patient as can be,
My every need she tries to meet,
For isn't *Jannah* beneath her feet?

Father who is strong and wise,
Does his utmost while he tries,
To be maintainer and protector too,
Like Almighty Allah told him to.

So next to Allah we then obey,
The Prophet, lest we go astray,
And never should we undermine,
Our parents who are next in line.

Our parents we can never repay,
For their welfare we must pray,
And try to make them happy too,
They are precious, that is true.

And Allah's words I always hear,
'In their old age keep them near,
Mercy and kindness you must show',
It's what everyone should know.

And your Lord has commanded that you should worship none but
Him, and show kindness to your parents.

(Bani-Israil 17:23)

# My Brother

I am the mirror of my brother,
And we care for one another,
To abuse him, is an evil act,
To fight him, is *Kufr* in fact.

His life and honour I do hold,
Sacred, like the Prophet told,
This includes possessions too,
It is what all of us should do.

My brother I would not defame,
Nor call him an offensive name,
In dealings I am always fair,
To show him that I truly care.

And how could I ever backbite,
And harm him or deny his right?
I love for him what I love for me,
Though sometimes we do not agree.

He and I should work together,
And be united now and forever,
For one thing must be understood,
All Muslims form a brotherhood!

# Eating Habits

Stop your play, it's time to eat,
Come wash your hands and take a seat,
Before you start though, bring to mind,
The mercy of Allah Who is so kind.

So begin in the name of Allah,
By always saying *Bismillah,*
Don't dish out more than you can eat,
For Muslims shouldn't over-eat.

And one thing you must understand,
It's good to eat with your right hand,
Never stuff your mouth with food,
That would surely be most rude.

Take your time and chew quite well,
Pick up morsels in case it fell,
Eat your food and leave no waste,
There's no need to eat in haste.

Drink your tea and sip it slow,
You don't have to gulp you know,
When you've finished thank Allah,
By always saying *Al-Hamdulillah.*

# Du'a before the meal

بِسْمِ اللهِ الرَّحْمٰنِ الرَّحِيْمُ

In the name of Allah the Merciful, the Compassionate.

# Du'a after the meal

اَلْحَمْدُ لِلّٰهِ الَّذِیْ اَطْعَمَنَا وَسَقَانَا وَجَعَلَنَا مِنَ الْمُسْلِمِیْنَ

Praise be to Allah Who gave us food, drink and made us Muslims.

# To Those Who Are Suffering

I dedicate this poem,
                to people everywhere,
Victims of oppression,
                showing that I care.
People just like us,
                who suffer all the time,
While they are not guilty,
                of any given crime.

Men and women young and old,
                living in despair,
They have to cope with laws,
                that simply are not fair.
And what about the children,
                suffering each day,
As their precious childhood,
                slowly slips away.

We must think of them,
                each passing day and night,
And do the best we can,
                to rid them of their plight.

'Please help us O Allah,
⠀⠀⠀⠀⠀⠀to be mindful and to care,
To reach out far and wide,
⠀⠀⠀⠀⠀⠀to help and do our share.'

# A Child's Prayer

I sometimes lie awake at night,
And wonder at the stars so bright,
I dream about my future too,
And the things that I will do.

Soon the nation will count on me,
I'm the future, they all agree,
And people depend on me somehow,
Though small and timid I am now.

So you and I, my dearest friend,
Must stand together till the end,
For we are one by Allah's Grace,
No matter what our creed or race.

We must prepare ourselves today,
While we journey on life's way,
So education, we must crave,
From the cradle to the grave.

So those entrusted with our care,
Train us please and do your share,
We'll make you proud of us somehow,
So waste no time and teach us now.

We need your love and tender care,
And your sincere and ardent prayer,
So much there is to learn and see,
For true believers we must be.

'O Allah, we do love You so,
Give us health and make us grow,
Be with us each passing day,
While we journey on life's way.'

# Glossary

**Akhirah:** The Hereafter, Next World, Life after Death: Muslims believe that Allah will reward and punish all human beings in the Next Life.

**Al-Hamdulillah:** The Arabic expression meaning 'Praise be to Allah'. Muslims say it for thanking Allah.

**Arafat:** The plain, 12 miles away from Makkah, where all pilgrims gather on the 9th Dhu'l-Hijjah.

**Arkan (plural of Rukn): Pillars:** The pillars of Islam are *Shahadah* (declaration of faith), Prayer, Fasting, Almsgiving and Pilgrimage.

**'Asr:** The third prayer of the day. Prayer performed in the late afternoon.

**Baitullah:** Allah's House (*Ka'bah*) built by the Prophets Ibrahim and Ismail (peace be upon them). Muslims pray facing towards it and visit it during the Pilgrimage.

**Bismillah:** The Arabic expression meaning 'In the name of Allah'. Muslims pronounce it before doing anything.

**Din:** Religion, covering all aspects of life.

**Fajr:** The first prayer of the day. Prayer performed at dawn, before sunrise.

**Fatihah:** The opening *Surah* (chapter) of the Qur'an recited in every Prayer.

**Hajj (Pilgrimage to Makkah):** Another pillar of Islam, a duty compulsory once in a lifetime for every Muslim who can afford it.

**'Ibadah:** Worship, service to God. Apart from ritual worship it includes all acts done for pleasing Allah and in fulfilling one's duties.

**'Id:** Festival. In Islam there are two *'Ids:* (1) *'Id al-Fitr* celebrated at the end of Ramadan and (2) *'Id al-Adha* on 10th - Dhu'l-Hijjah marking the culmination of the *Hajj.*

**Ihram:** A ritual dress worn by pilgrims during the Pilgrimage.

**Iman:** Faith, religious belief.

46

*'Isha':* The fifth and last prayer performed in the late evening.

**Islam:** The final religion, way of life prescribed by Allah for mankind. Literally it means: 'submission, peace'.

*Jahannam* **(Hell):** Those who do bad/evil deeds in this life would be sent to Hell for punishment.

*Jannah* **(Paradise):** Those who do good deeds in this life would be admitted by Allah to Paradise as a reward.

*Kufr:* Unbelief, rejection of Islam, wrong-doing.

*Lailatul-Qadr:* One of the last five odd nights of Ramadan which the Qur'an describes as a 'blessed night'. Muslims perform extra prayers on this night.

*Maghrib:* The fourth prayer performed after sunset.

**Muslim:** A follower of Islam. One who has submitted himself fully to the Will of Allah.

*Qiblah:* The direction of the *Ka'bah* in Makkah, facing which Muslims pray all over the world.

**Qur'an:** The Word of Allah revealed to the Prophet Muhammad (peace be upon him). It is the final source of all teachings, commands and guidance in Islam.

*Rak'ah:* One cycle of the Prayer.

*Ramadan:* The ninth month of the Islamic calendar. Muslims fast throughout this month as thanksgiving for Allah's sending down of the Qur'an during this month.

*Rukn:* Pillar (see *Arkan*).

*Ruku':* The posture of bowing down in the Prayer.

*Sa'i:* A ritual of the Pilgrimage; running 7 times between Safa and Marwah in Makkah.

*Salah* **(Prayers):** Five daily prayers are compulsory for every Muslim adult.

*Sawm:* Fasting in the month of Ramadan between dawn and sunset which is compulsory for every Muslim adult.

*Shahadah (La ilaha illallah Muhammad-ur-Rasulullah):* Literally it means: 'There is no god but Allah and Muhammad is Allah's Messenger'. This declaration of faith is the first pillar of Islam.

*Sujud* **(plural of** *Sajdah***):** Prostration during the Prayer.

**Sunnah:** The practice of the Prophet Muhammad (peace be upon him).

**Takbir (Allah Akbar):** It means 'Allah is Great', said before and during the Prayer.

**Taqwa:** Having an awareness and fear of Allah.

**Tawaf:** Going round the *Ka'bah* in a ritual way.

**Tawhid:** Oneness of God. It is the basic belief in Islam that Allah alone deserves all worship and obedience.

**Wudu (Ablution):** Ritual washing before the Prayer.

**Zakah:** Compulsory Alms; one of the five pillars of Islam.

**Zuhr:** The second prayer performed in early afternoon.

# Vocabulary

**Books:** It refers to Allah's Message sent down in different ages through His Messengers. Torah and Gospel (Bible) are the earlier books which have been replaced by Allah's final Message - the Qur'an revealed to the Prophet Muhammad (peace be upon him).

**Brotherhood:** Feelings of love and kindness for others for the sake of pleasing Allah.

**Divine:** Something sent by Allah.

**Judgement Day:** The Last Day when all human beings will be judged and rewarded or punished according to their deeds.

**Mercy (Qur'an):** One of the names of the Qur'an. Being Allah's Guidance, it is a great blessing for all of mankind.

**Right Way (Straight Path):** The Way shown by Allah through the Qur'an and the Prophet.

**Sign (Qur'an):** As the sign the Qur'an points to the existence and presence of Allah everywhere in the universe.

**Trustee:** Someone in charge of something or entrusted with some responsibility. According to the Qur'an, man's position in the world is that of a trustee; he is expected to use all his talents and energy for obeying God's commands and for trying to win His pleasure.